OAK CRADLE

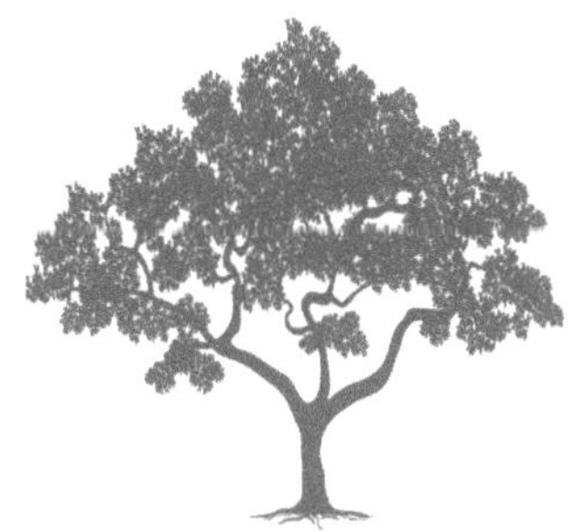

OAK CRADLE

poetry by

Chantel L. Carlson

photography by

Karen D. Gros

SHANTI ARTS PUBLISHING
BRUNSWICK, MAINE

OAK CRADLE

Published by Shanti Arts Publishing

Designed by Shanti Arts Designs

Shanti Arts LLC
193 Hillside Road
Brunswick, Maine 04011
shantiarts.com

Printed in the United States of America

ISBN: 978-1-962082-19-8 (softcover)

Library of Congress Control Number: 2023950767

In Loving Memory of Garrett Velasquez

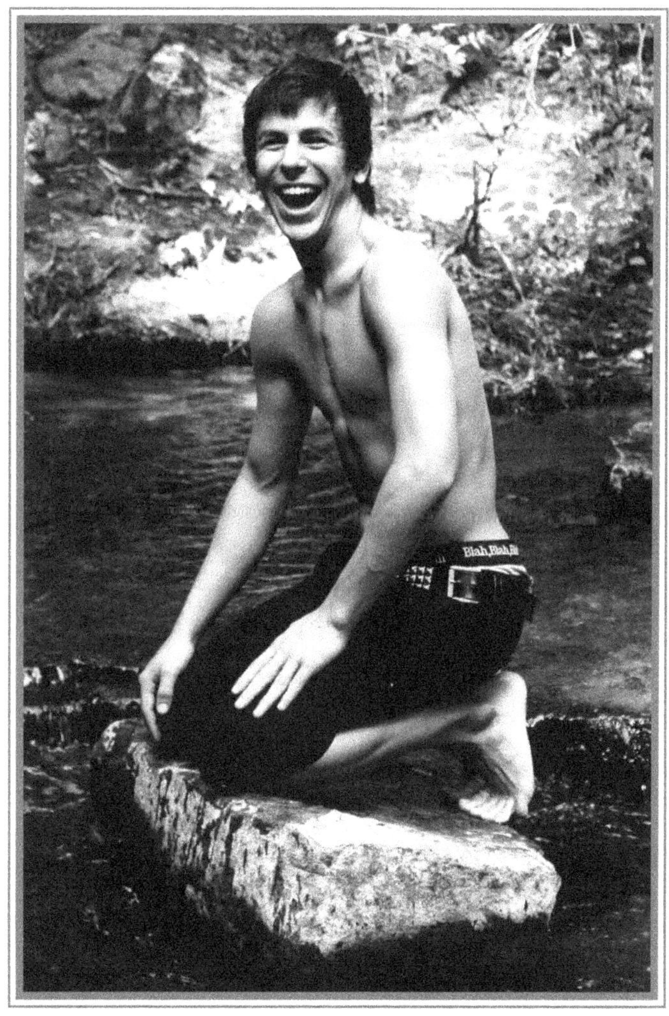

November 24, 1992 – September 19, 2011

CONTENTS

THE BEGINNING 11

I. THE BURIAL

ON WITH THE SHOW 15
CHOKING CANARY 17
A MOTHER'S GRIEF 18
THE SOUVENIR 20
THE CHASE 23
AWAKENING 24
LEARNING HOW TO LIVE AGAIN 26
EMBERS 28
FERMATA 31
WHY I NAMED MY HEART MATADOR 32
ODE TO THE BACKYARD DOVE 34

II. HOLDING THE DEAD INTO EXISTENCE

RECKONING 38
METAMORPHOSIS 41
THE SPARROW 43
THE CHARM OF REVELATION 44
BON RÊVES 46
BEFORE THE RAIN 49

III. RESURRECTION

ON THE ANNIVERSARY OF MY SON'S DEATH 53
A REPRIEVE 54
THE PRAYER 56
ALL OUT, ALL OVER 58
RESURRECTION 61

ACKNOWLEDGMENTS 65
DEDICATIONS 67
ABOUT THE POET AND PHOTOGRAPHER 71

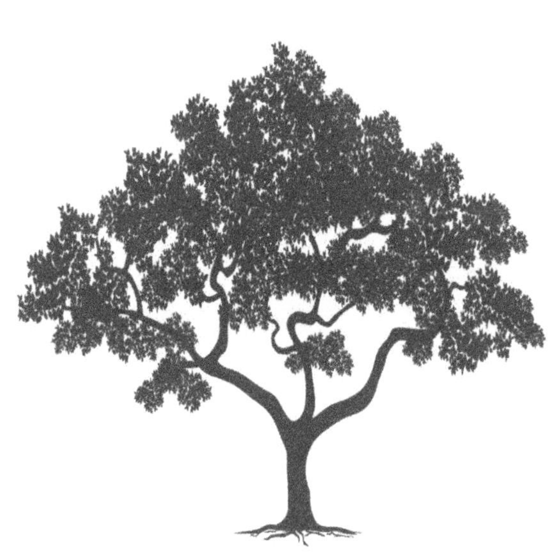

THE BEGINNING

Back in 2015 I was scrolling through my social media feed and stumbled across a series of images taken by my cousin Karen D. Gros. All of them featured a woman in black, a woman in mourning. Having experienced some personal losses of my own, I was immediately drawn to her.

Karen told me that the woman was Emily Knobloch, a family friend, and that these photographs were taken in Emily's family home in Thibodaux, Louisiana in May 2011. Karen used objects she found in their attic, including old photos and furniture that belonged to the family. The chest Emily is photographed in (page 14) is from the early 1800s and still contained a black linen mourning dress, the one she wore in the photos.

What Karen never could have predicted is that ninety days after these images were taken, her nineteen-year-old son, Garrett, would die by suicide. He drove his car head on into an oak tree. Karen literally became the mourning woman in the images, and her photography became a way for her to cope with this unimaginable loss. She once told me, "I wonder if this all was fate. 'Life imitates art' comes to mind . . . I think once I knew the dress was a mourning dress, I had a vision. I question the motive behind many of the photos that day, as they certainly tell my story today."

This project is a visual and written narrative following the journey of a woman through grief, loss, and perseverance. Because the grieving process can often cause isolation and the feeling that you are the only one experiencing this type of pain, our hope for this project is that it opens up a dialogue about grief and reminds our audience that they are not alone.

I

THE BURIAL

I want to postpone the moment of ending, and in this way delude myself into thinking that I have only just begun, that the better part of my story still lies ahead. No matter how useless these words might seem to be, they have nevertheless stood between me and a silence that continues to terrify me. When I step into this silence, it will mean [he] has vanished forever.

—Paul Auster, *The Invention of Solitude*

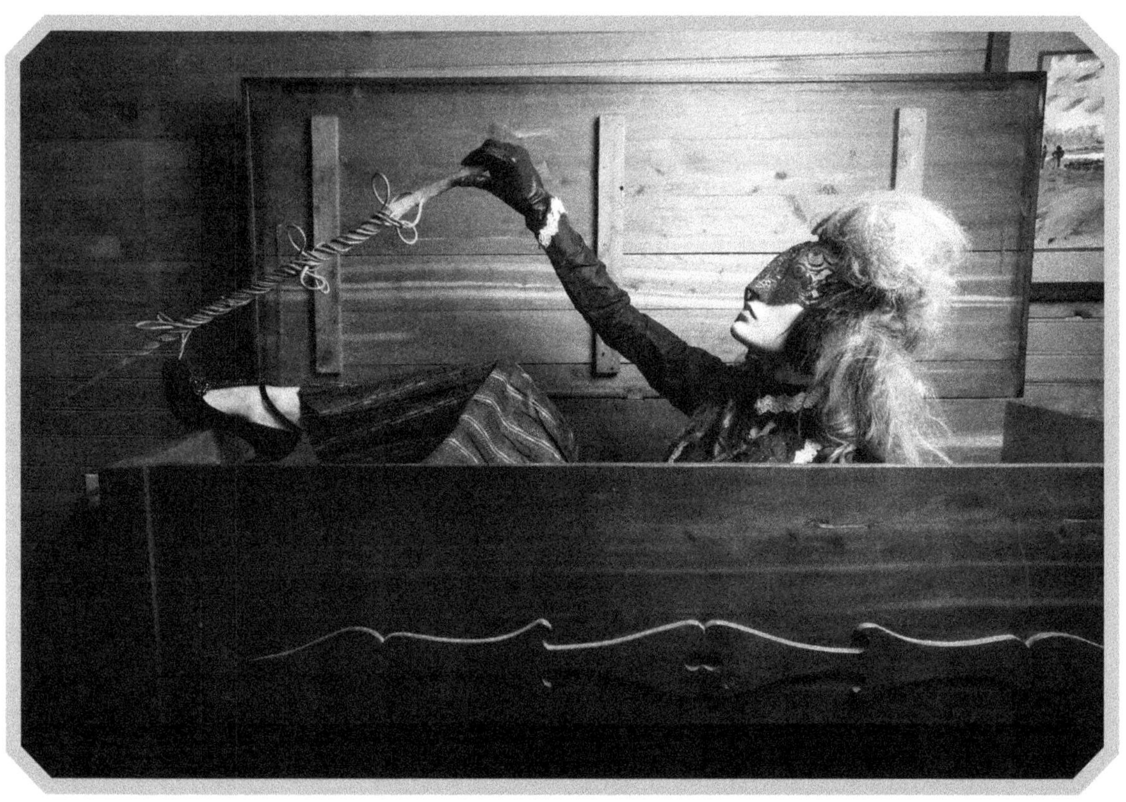

ON WITH THE SHOW

"Ladies and gentlemen,
children of all ages,

come see the lady in black
for one night only as she performs

her grief without a safety net.
Come see this creature emerge

to reveal her white-knuckled grips
for breath when death lights

the fuse of the rubber-spring cannon
and she becomes a cycling

cyclone whirring 180 degrees until
she proceeds to fall."

Every night's the same.

I lift the lid when calliope's tune
accelerates through compressed air—

large locomotive whistles, gasps
for air through brass pipes.

When my body is in full view,
I spin in visions and revisions

of death and division, waiting
for the applause to inspirit

this chamber. Every night
I'm swallowed in silence.

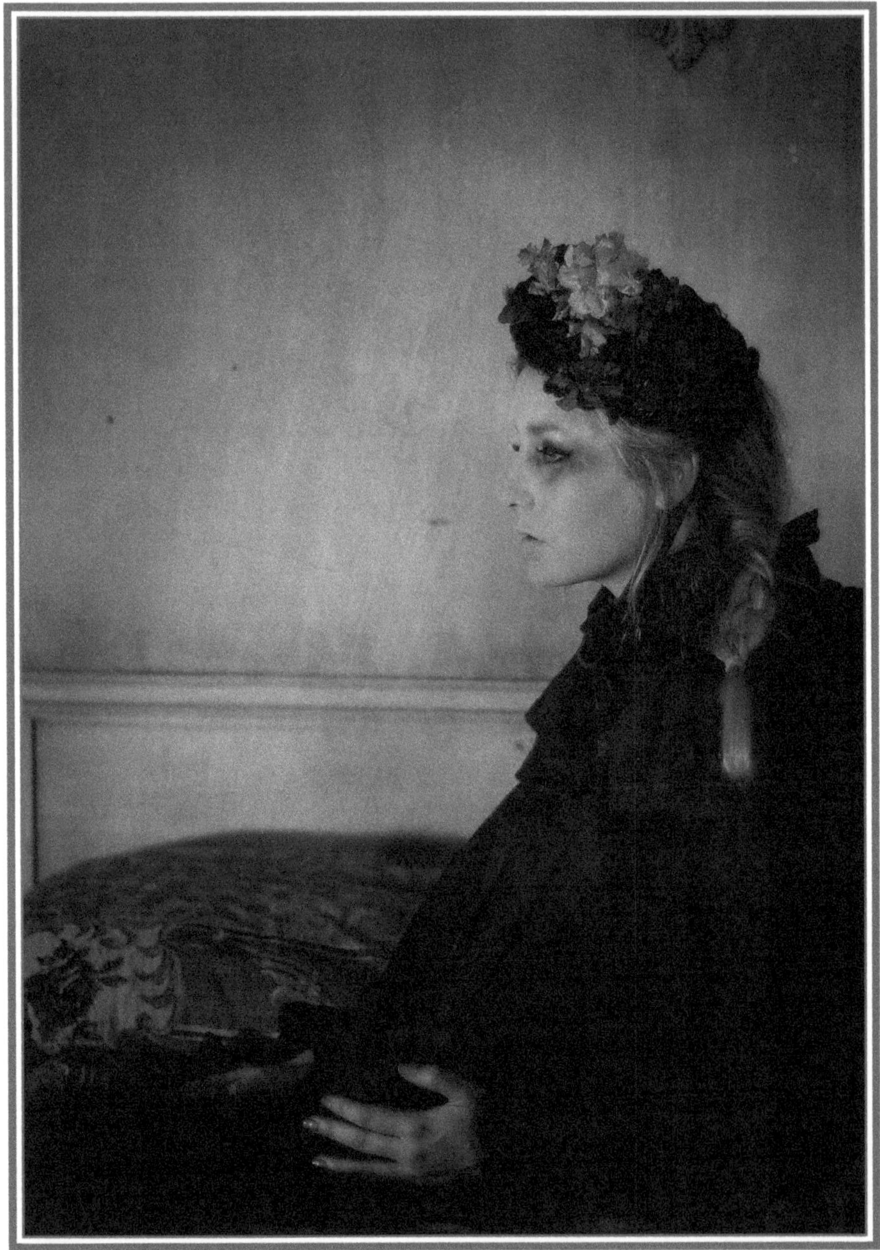

CHOKING CANARY

All I have left
are ghosts gasping down the hall
when my knees capsize
and I fall into grief's refrain
of bereaved geographies:
the easy breeze of moss, green
shudders in sway and oyster shells
cracking beneath my feet. Submerged
in Gulf heat, my fingers bleed
spearmint onto Avenue A where I
played hide and seek with my son,
his soft breath still
brushing his chest. I remember
when death didn't know where we lived,
and we ate mustard greens and tomatoes
bright as the worm moon climbing up
an oak's bark marked by every storm.

A MOTHER'S GRIEF

I look through glass blinking
the moonlight, my mind buried

with you in the coffin.
I give in to the ache tearing

tendrils and tendons choking
each blink and breath. I clutch

my womb rotting at the roots,
thinning canopies with no remedy

but to remove. I want to live
where you live, but the limbs

of the oak cradle you instead.
If you shed a tear in the ocean,

I'd drown in search of
the drop that belonged to you.

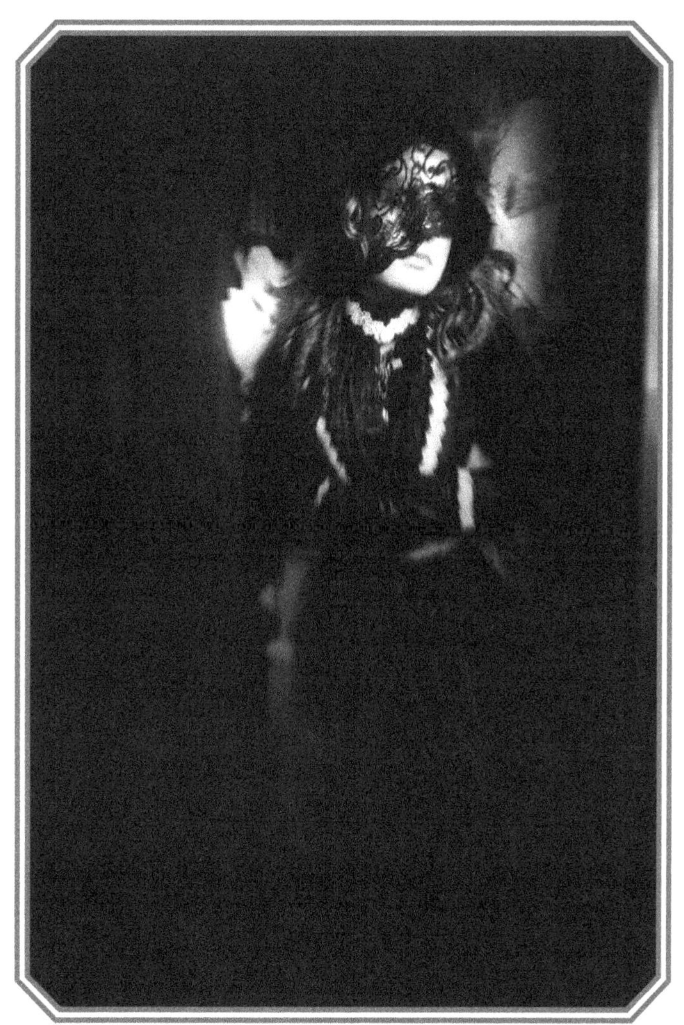

THE SOUVENIR

My son stands on Bourbon
where humid air drips in each crack
of decayed Spanish wood.
He heralds me into a mask store,
asks me to pick one out. He wants me
to remember the day beads of sweat traced
the edges of my shoulders, down my back,
a Rorschach form of an ocean's crest
tipped with white foam
hissing in the wind.
As we step off asphalt and walk inside,
the heat reaches for our feet
begging to burn this day into our skin.
I study the porcelain faces:
ribbon hair sails like curled masts at the end,
mouths agape, swallowing the taste
of jazz on their pursed lips that will chip
by year's end. I begin
to finger each cheek as he reaches
for a heart-shaped face, divided
black and white like the posturing
wings of the Mississippi kite.
His ash hair smells like magnolias
and the chicory coffee he drank
at 3 am in our lemon kitchen.
"This one," he says.
I would have chosen differently,
but because he touches it with his own hand,
still warm, still here, I know
it is the only one I ever wanted.

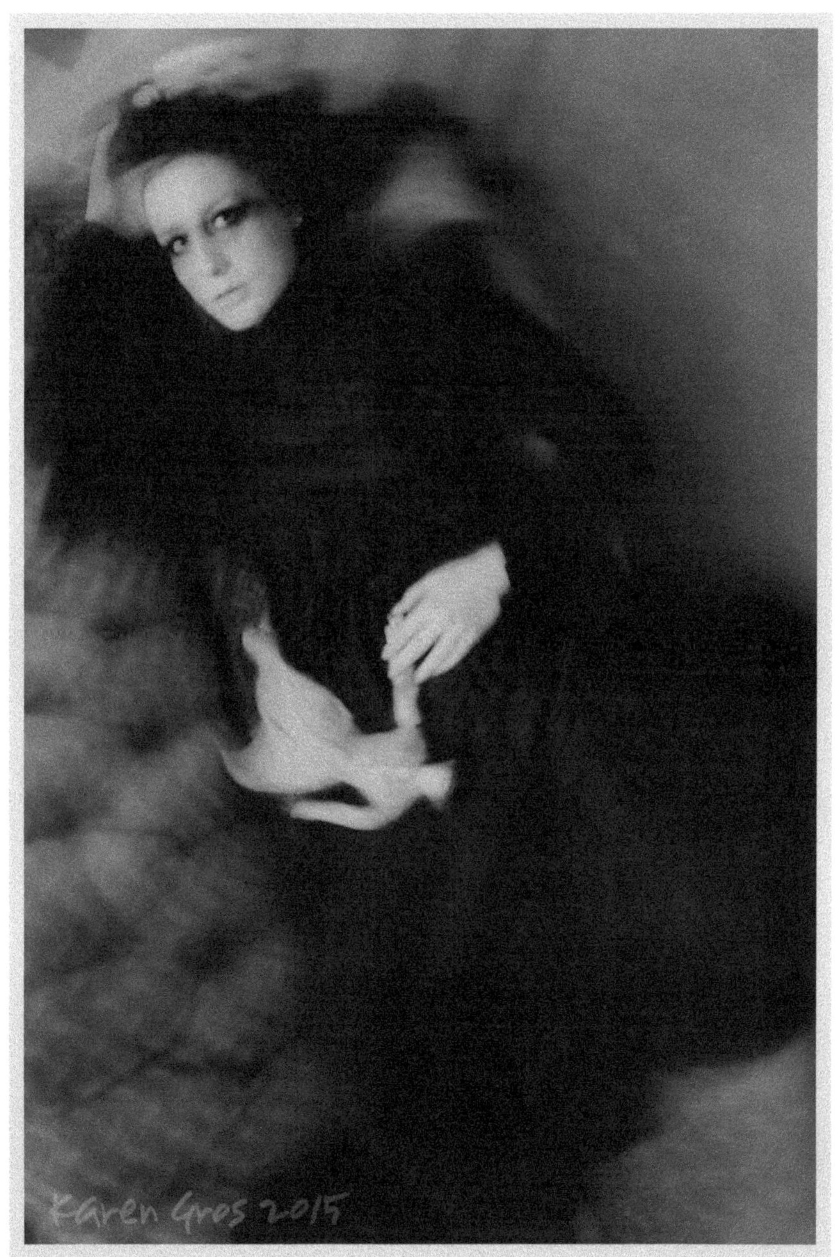
Karen Gros 2015

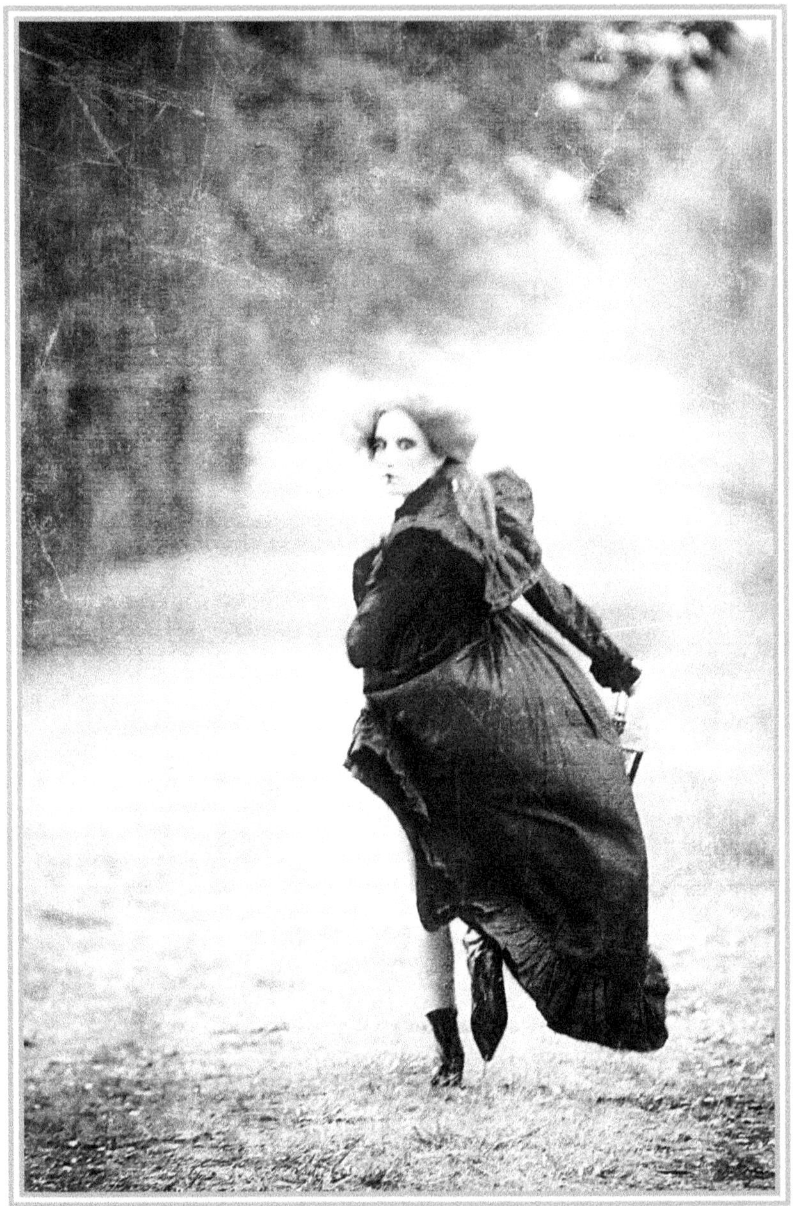

THE CHASE

I can't run from death
cloaked in, choked in

this black mourning fog.
I am the mad woman

wound and bound in yellow
wallpaper. I'll scratch

my way out, out into
this field where grief howls

from its hollow jowl.
I run uncovered

through a void of stars
and skies scarred from death.

I stop—see you wave
your sickle over graves.

AWAKENING

I hear the oak begin
to cry so I walk

through fettered fog to dry
the drops from each leaf

I trace margin to rib
to netted veins

to sing summer still
reaching in leaves

where there is no breath
in the broken, I begin

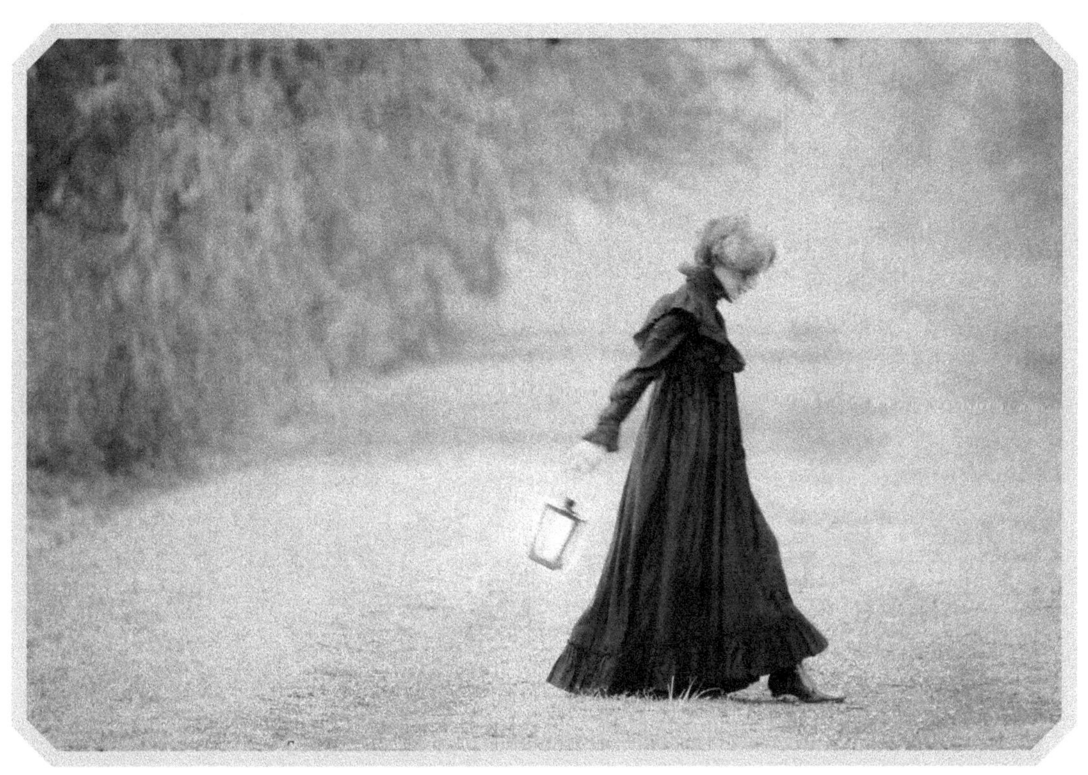

LEARNING HOW TO LIVE AGAIN

Bourbon blues move
tourist shoes through concrete

beat, beat down the Quarter.
Fortune tellers feeling dollars,

compelling fathers to open
palms, promising farther

than the eye can. See I've known
these streets, owned these streets

in younger days, but now
I struggle through memory's haze

to remember:
the smells of, swells of,

swinging Jackson bells
of backtracking thoughts,

Creole air thick, stick
on my skin. Loved ones

who walked me through,
talked me through, are now

shadows upon shadows slipping
through voodoo alleys

to Aunt Sally's to the square steeple.
I'll sit on steps as jazz sways

the breeze, breathe in ease,
and lean into lantern light.

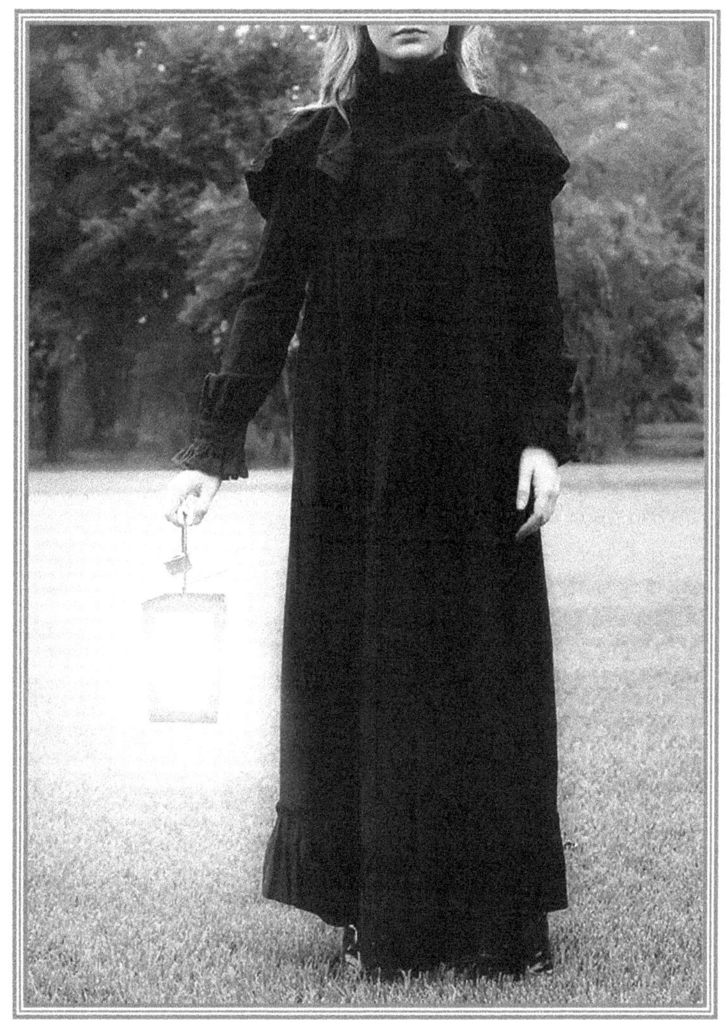

EMBERS

My womb is now
an aching tomb

I place my grief inside
a lantern, encase your light

so I will always carry
a piece of you

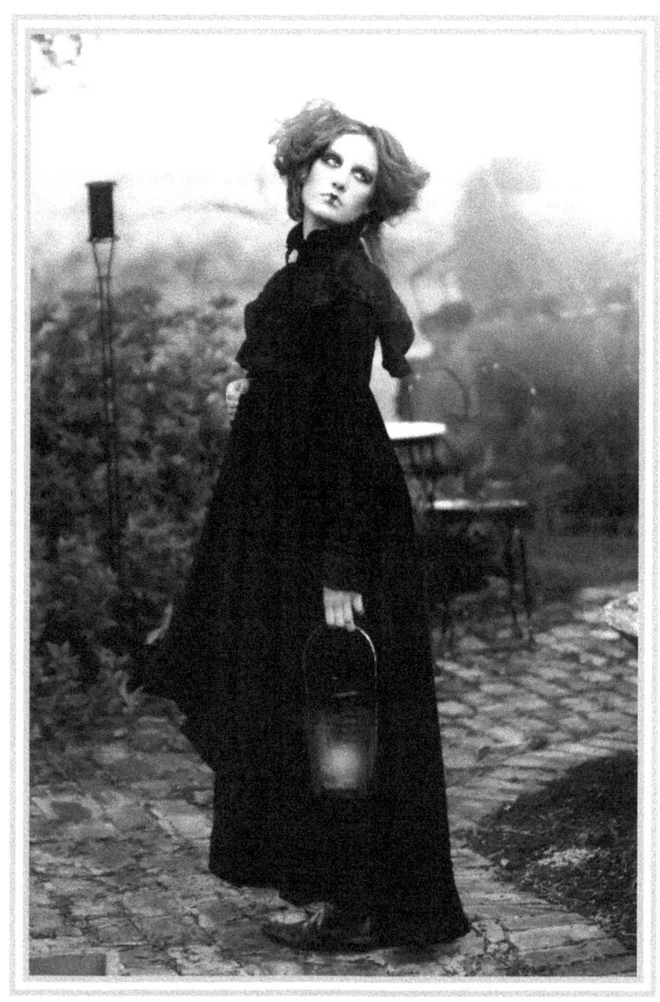

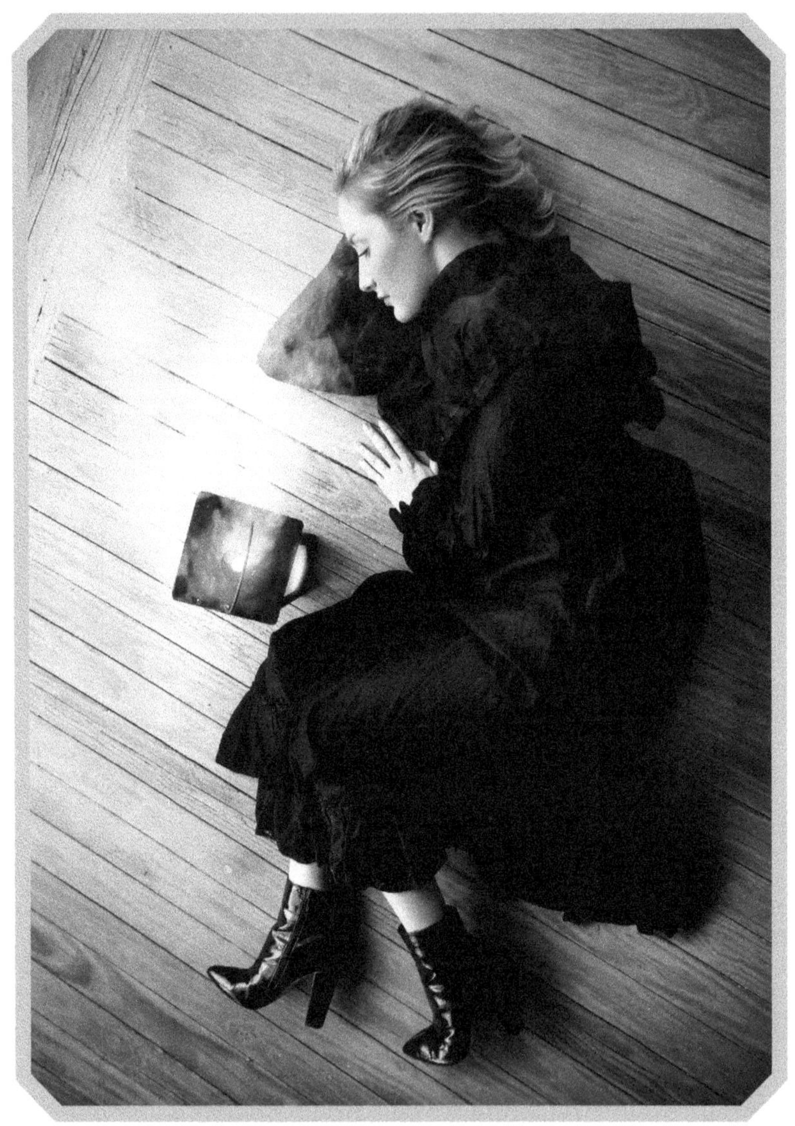

FERMATA

And now I've come to rest,
like the pause before

the next second, or the cypress
knees that breathe in rising water.

I think of you inside these spaces.
The way these trees release the dead

needled leaves on rust-colored walkways,
and the wind holds them in a spin.

I lie and wait palm over palm
pressed against my chest, until

someone reaches over to open
the lantern, and extinguish the light.

WHY I NAMED MY HEART MATADOR

Because today I stood at the foot
of my son's grave when the sun set

red nightshades over my face.
And when I came home, I stopped

and looked into a mirror only to see
a woman cloaked in grief. But

soon I will walk barefoot
through junipers, pick pentas

and smell its sweet. Soon
I will take the cape and stand

in the ring when grief begins
to charge my heart. I will

plant my toes in the sinking sand
and continue to hold on.

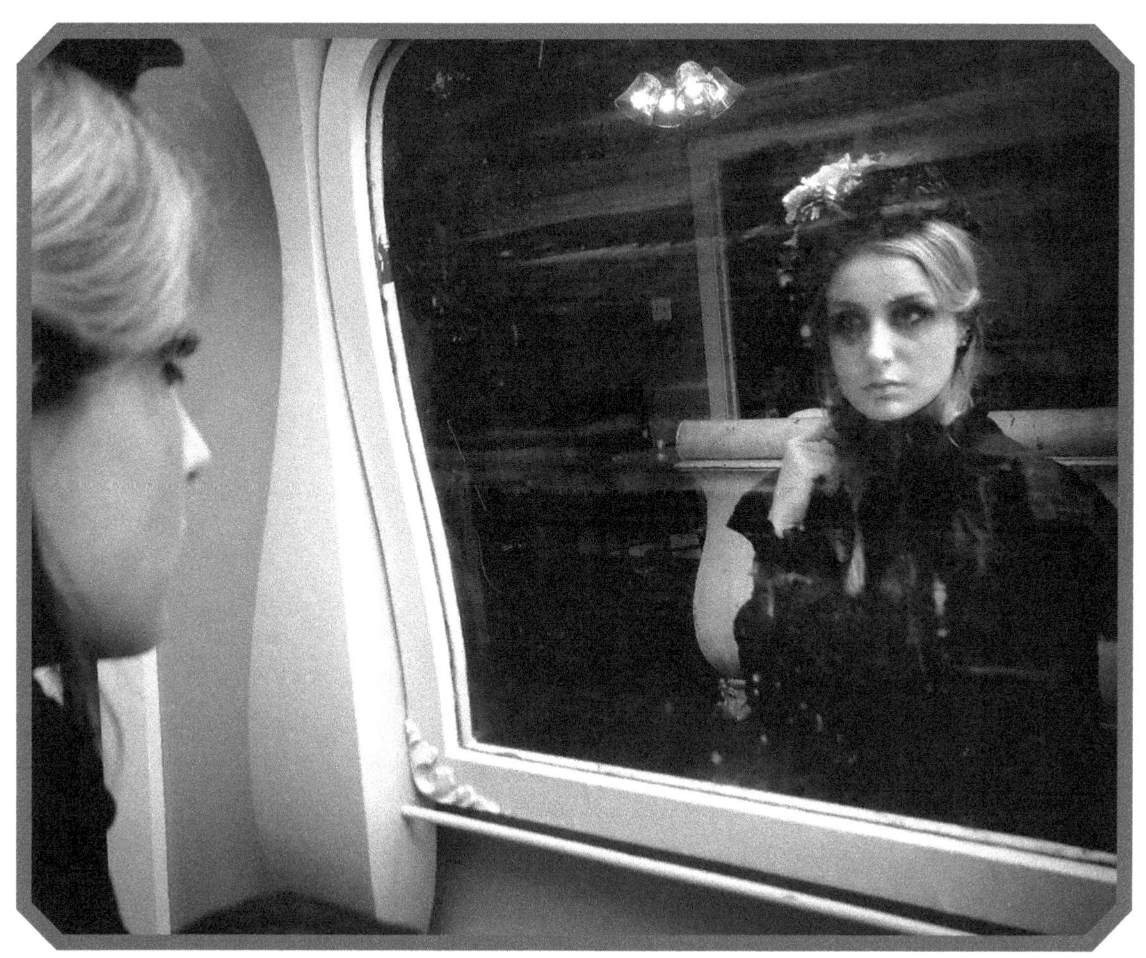

ODE TO THE BACKYARD DOVE

I know you don't always mourn.
During early dawn, I see you
perambulate across the wooden feeder
rocking back and forth like you're
on an abandoned seesaw,
waiting. You claim the fresh
seed as your own:
the sunflower, the safflower, the cracked corn.
Let it fall from the tip of your beak
onto the ground to root
into something green.
And when you've had your fill, you
shift your rounded belly surrounding
those talons creased beneath to ground
yourself against the approaching storm.
I love how you hold on in spite of it all.
I love how your cadence carries in triple time,
each time. How I'll come back
this time tomorrow and see you still
there wanting more.
I know you don't always mourn.

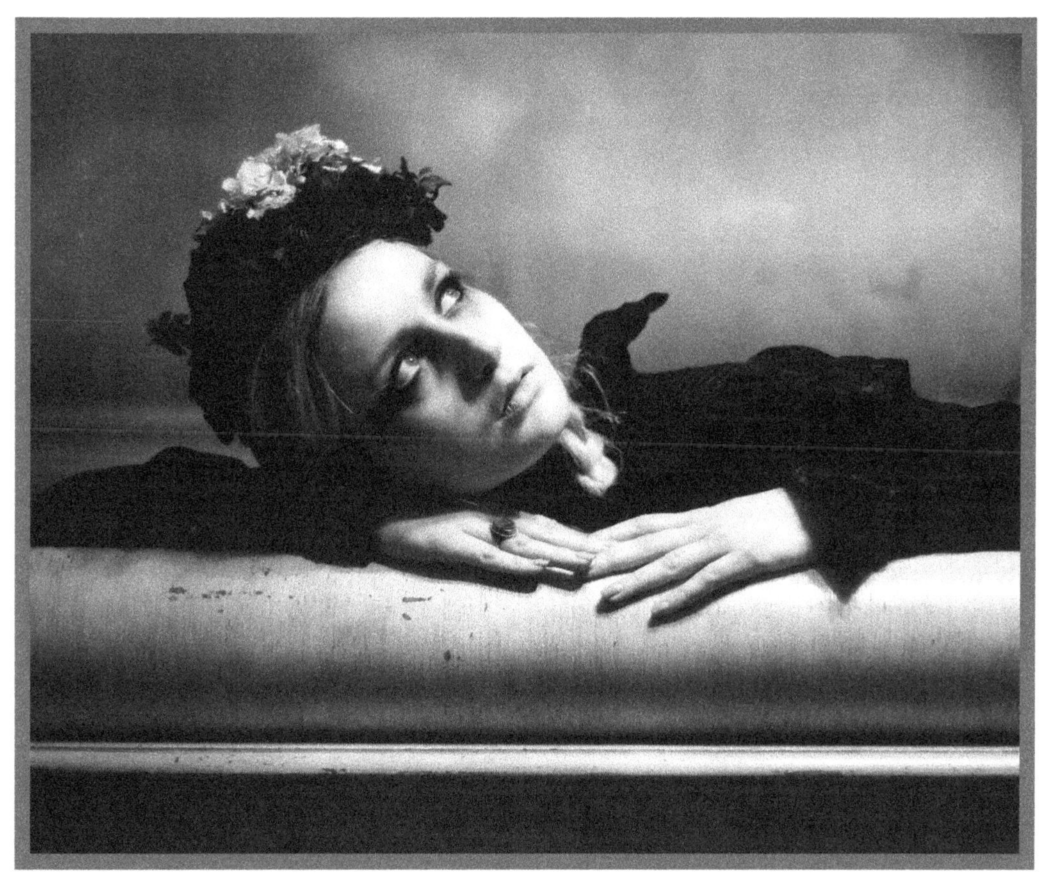

II

HOLDING THE DEAD INTO EXISTENCE

Give me that stupid, reliable cloud
because it might be the only thing
that never leaves . . .

Give me that cloud.
Give me this ache that lets me know
I'm alive.

—Megan Falley, "Rain"

RECKONING

Today's the day
I'll stare Death in the face,

maggots dripping down
her melted lips, mouth

agape, where black tar
snakes down skeleton

tooth and jaw. As fear
begins to thaw, I cross

arm to arm no longer
charmed by her offer

to end time this time.
This time I'll stay unafraid.

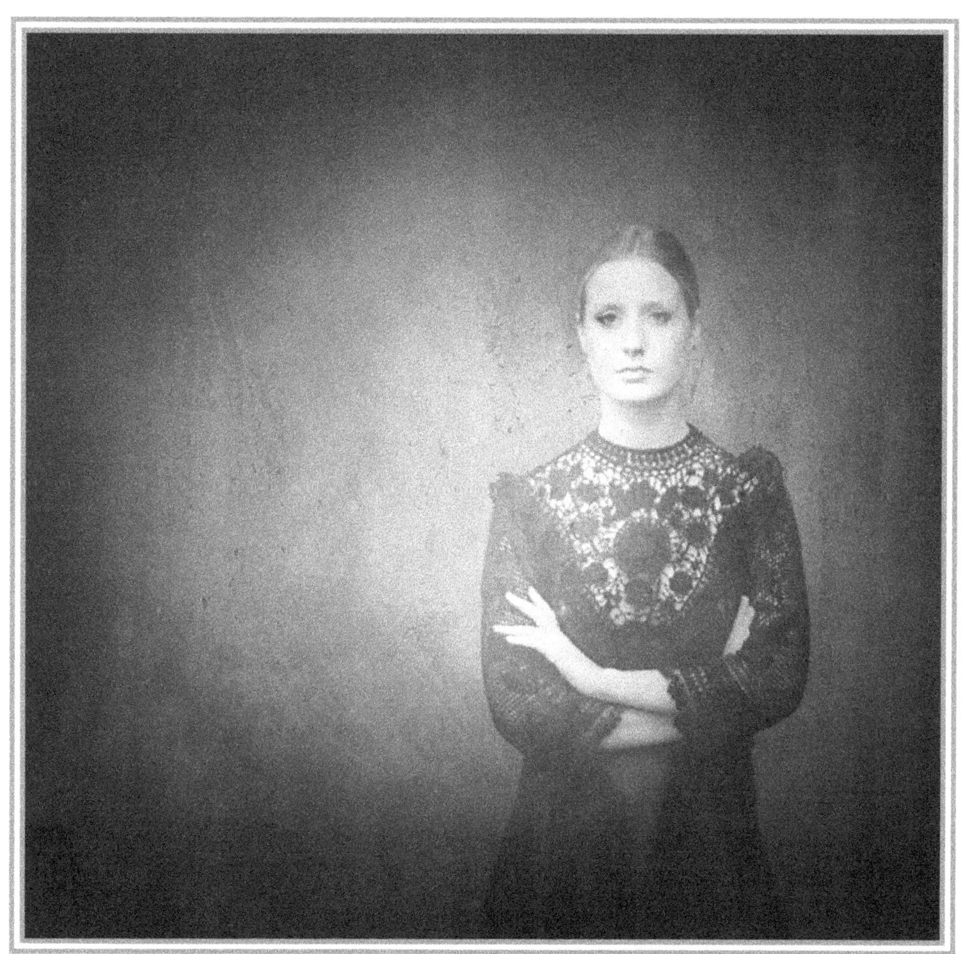

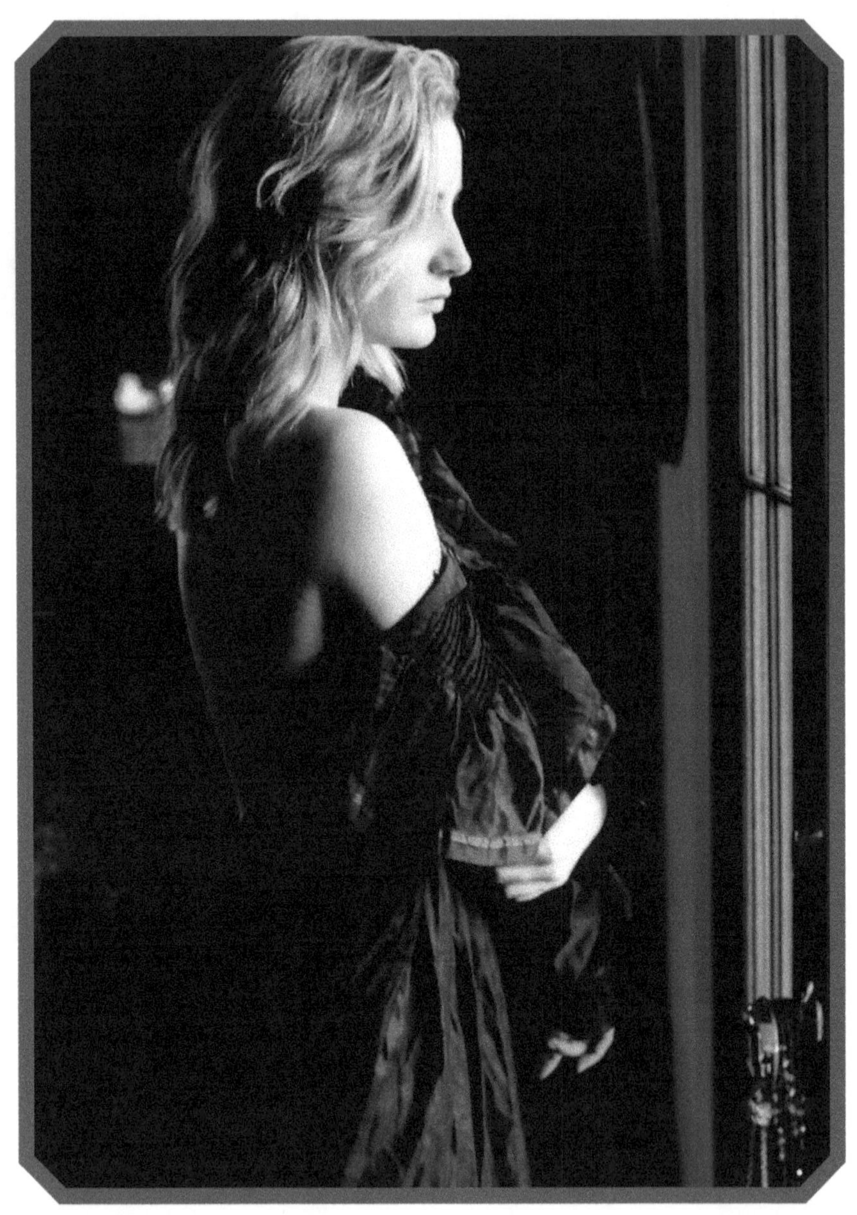

METAMORPHOSIS

Past time and rain on the window's
stillness, my gaze turns

to blue. Quilled in blue seeped through
to vein the blood with ink

no longer dry. My gaze turns
to skin, Rorschach forms:

oaks and daggers and ships sail
across lifelines once held

in a gypsy's palm. The bourbon
moon never tasted so good.

My gaze turns to shut ticks
and stocks of time-crossed

memory. Drawn feathered.
Drawn blue.

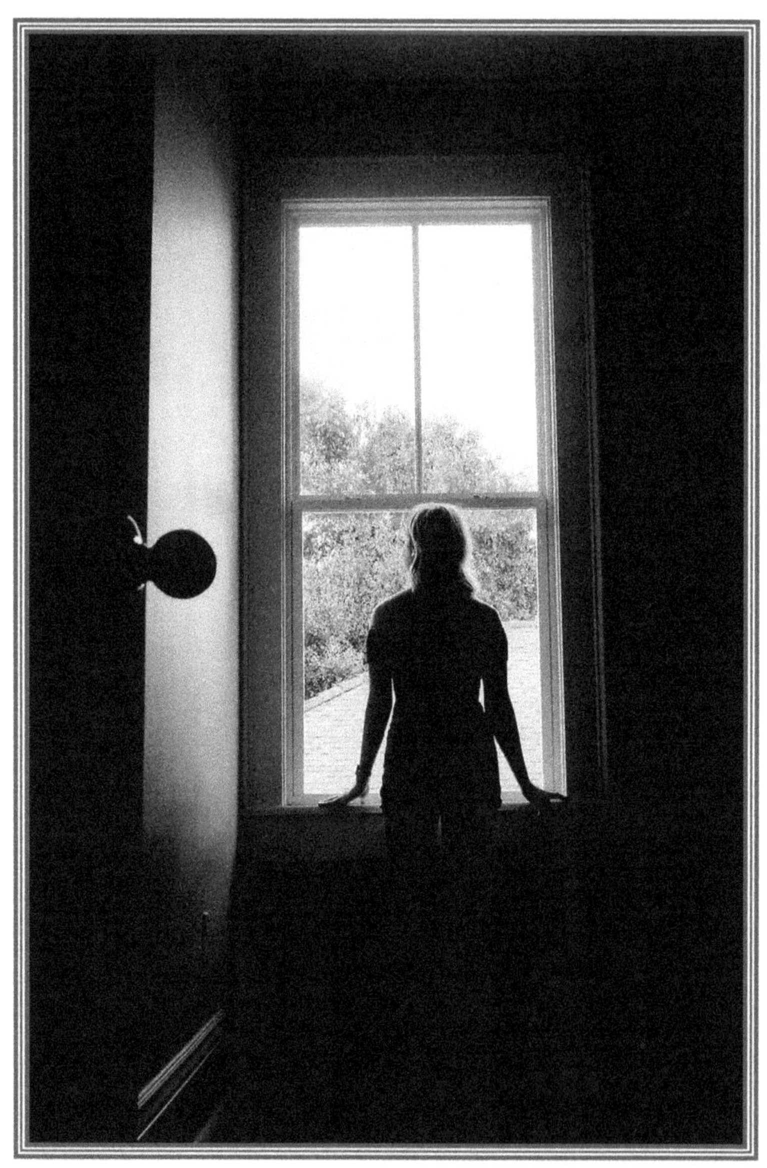

THE SPARROW

Today a sparrow narrowed its focus
to my windowpane.

Her reflection attacks back
over and over,

like a reel that flaps in on itself
at the projected end. But no one

comes to turn off the switch.
I lick my lips to remind myself

I'm human. Remind myself
I haven't died doing the same

beating against the unbreakable.
I watch her breathe slow

until only the wind moves
through her feathers

lifting stripes and streaks
on her outstretched neck.

It's no longer worth
the broken wing.

THE CHARM OF REVELATION

how many times / more excruciating / the charm of /revelation . . .
—Marthe Reed

My son tries to hold water in his hand,
asks why the sand swallows
what is his. A fiddler crab
throws quartz and mica minerals
in his face like it's celebrating
its ability to escape life.
I know there's safety in pebbled
darkness. I know constellations
can never reach the ocean.
But when the rain starts to fall,
I still believe I can touch
the palm of Cassiopeia
without angering the sea.

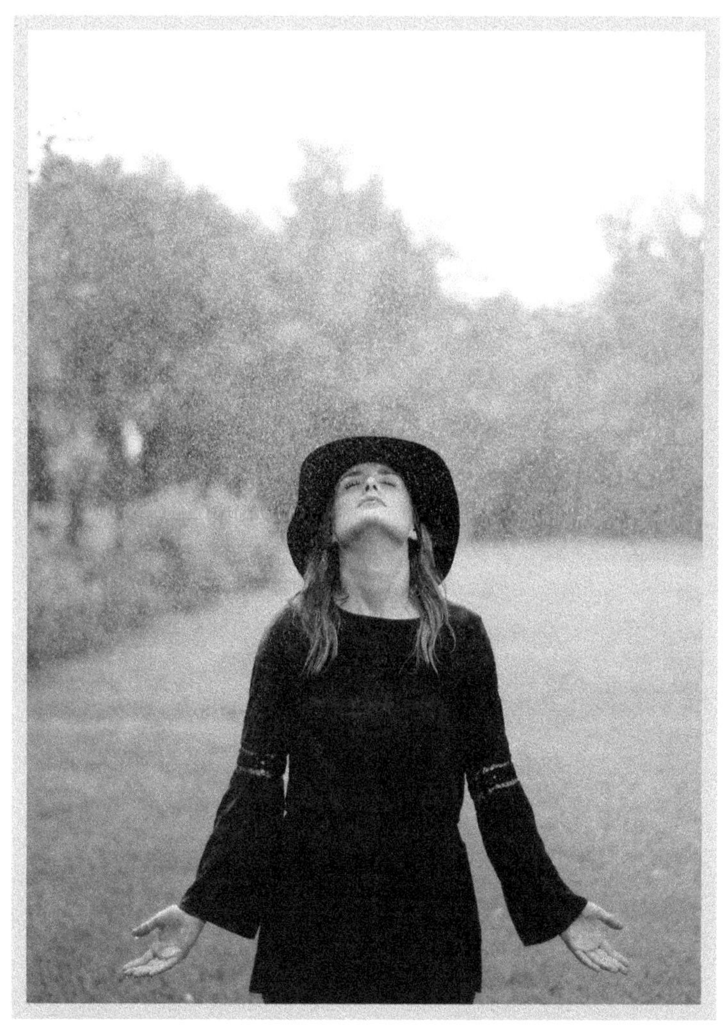

BON RÊVES

Summer cicadas scream
in 200-year-old oak leaves

down Magnolia St. off Amis.
June bugs scratch on porch doors

beneath a carport before
falling flat on their backs.

Their stick legs catch
the rhythm of bayou blues.

Smoke fills the air from sugar cane
burning in the fields.

My grandfather once said,
Il ne dure pas longtemps

but I still remember
the first sweet bite in his garden

guarded by the memory
of summers in Louisiana.

As the sun sets, the trees fall silent—
Écoutez

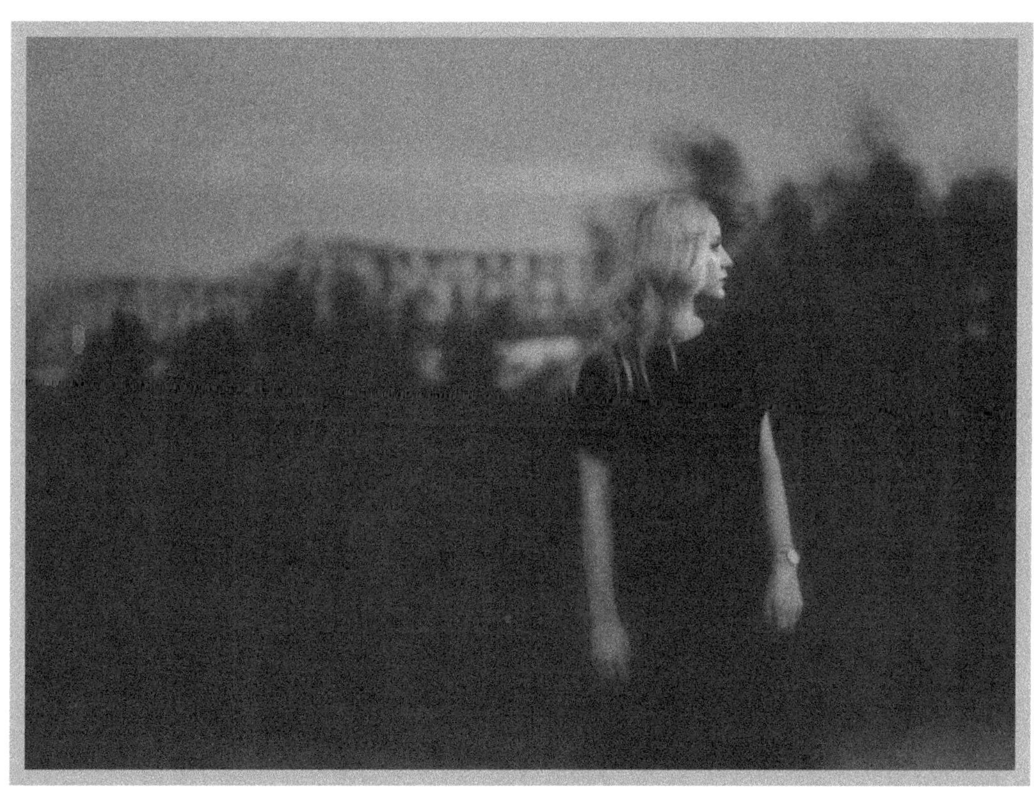

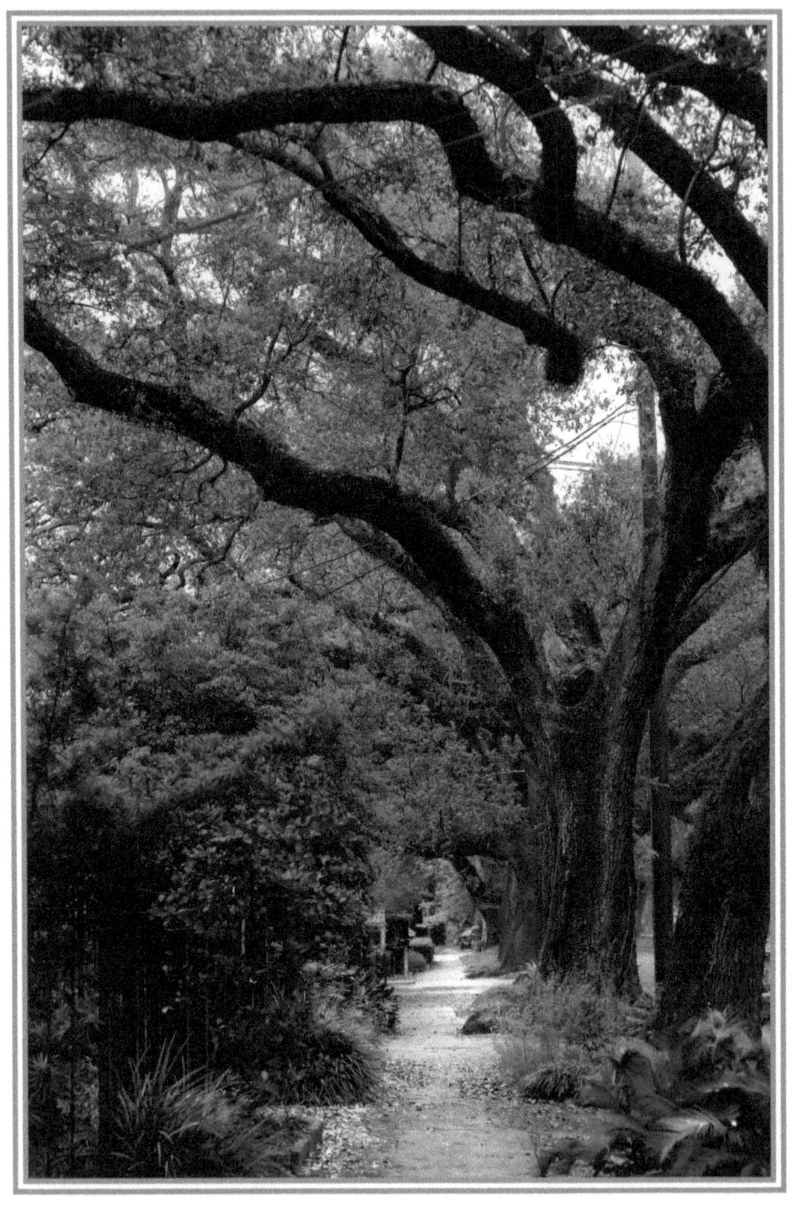

BEFORE THE RAIN

I walk down cracked sidewalks
off Birch Street, where cast iron

plants thrive in spite of neglect
burned into each edge.

As I round St. Charles,
the breeze seeds sounds

of mules clucking their bridled teeth
and trumpets echoing through Canal

and the streetcar bell arrival.
I clink change from my palm

and wade through each empty
aisle, one in front of the other.

I watch oak after oak claim a corner,
where old leaves drop from lateral

limbs in the same syncopated rhythm
as the year my son was still alive.

III

RESURRECTION

You see: light escapes from a body at night
and in the morning, despite the oppressive vacancy
of her leaving's shadow, light comes up
over the mountains and it is and it is and it is.

—Ada Limón, "Relentless"

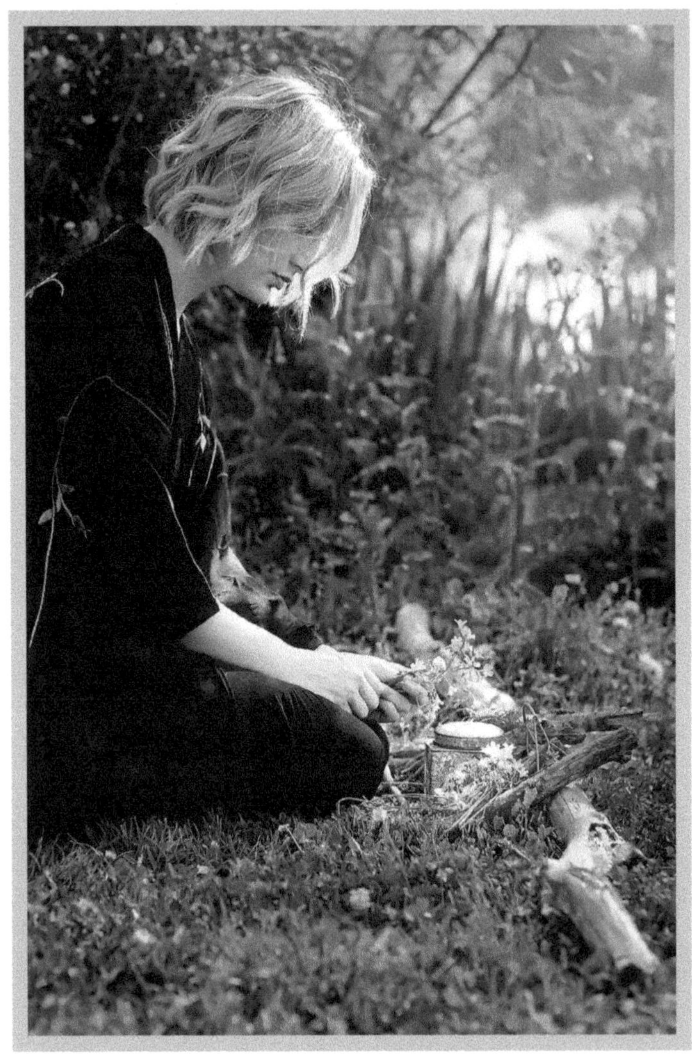

ON THE ANNIVERSARY OF MY SON'S DEATH

I stand under the broken
oak and peel a piece of rotting bark.
I brush dust from my fingers

in a back-and-forth rhythm
onto the head of the dead
cicada that lies at my feet,

its striped abdomen no longer
collapsing to sing summer heat,
legs suspended in the air.

I use an empty matchstick box
to bury him in a bed of cotton,
a breathable textile where there is

no breath. When I close the box,
a chorus begins to vibrate in leaves
one body at a time.

A REPRIEVE

Lone home in gray grass I
scratch to find

the surface after my child
died in the street.

I lie back in the grass
and feel fear brush over.

I wonder if he watches now
from open windows. I wait

for him to open the door
and call my name.

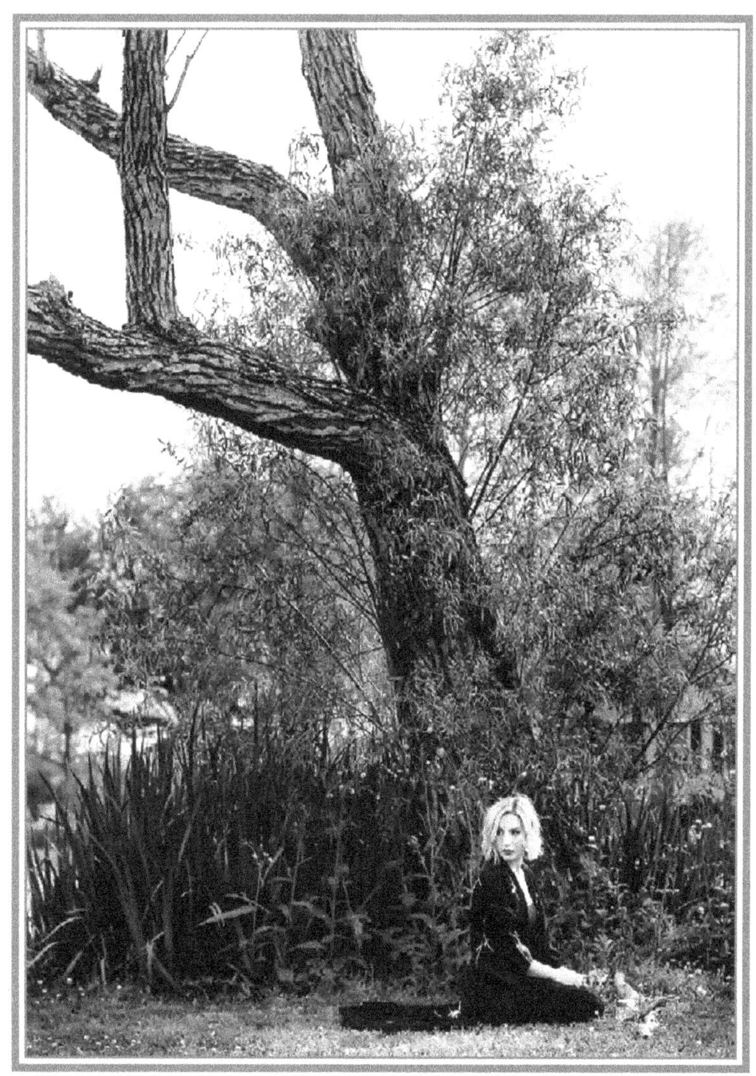

THE PRAYER

I'll clip clop Bourbon down
black concrete hot beneath
my feet. Breathe the thick
Mississippi air that makes
anyone's hair stick against
damp cheek. Watch me pass
green and white awnings
with bridled blues down,
down Toulouse. I've witnessed
prayer beads save believers.
Palm readers and fortune tellers
feel futures with their fingers.
An abandoned man turns
a church step into a pillow,
awaits his entrance against
a locked door. His hand rests
beside his temple where
it fell somewhere between
the name of the father and the son.
I walk away and hear him whisper
a prayer that all he wants
is to be home.

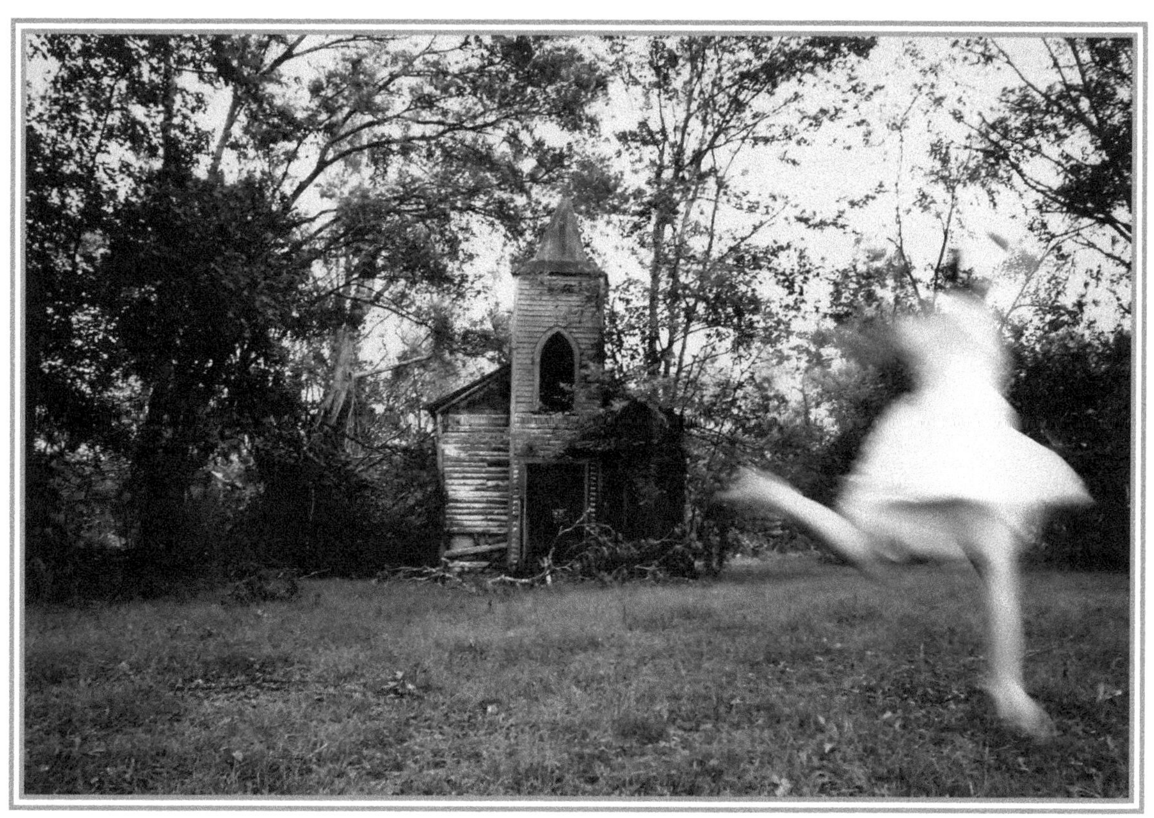

ALL OUT, ALL OVER

And so the show comes
to a close. Empty shells
shucked for peanuts are
swept in receptacles,
ticket stubs abandoned
like crepe myrtle petals
in rain. And when
the calliope steam sinks
in the night, blown like ash
remains cast downwind
in an acrobatic motion before
falling safely to the ground,
I'll pretend it was worth
the standing ovation. I'll
pretend I can place my grief
and the comfort of memory
in the same place before closing
the lid of the coffin, concealing
beneath the satin ceiling
each story of ghosts I knew.

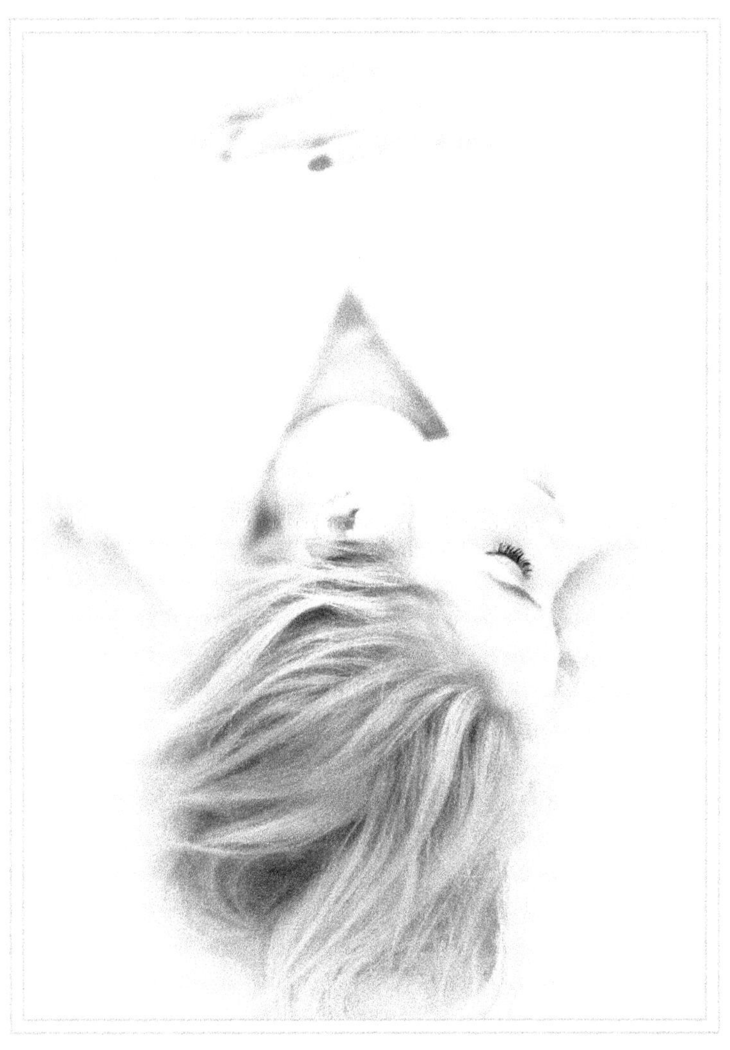

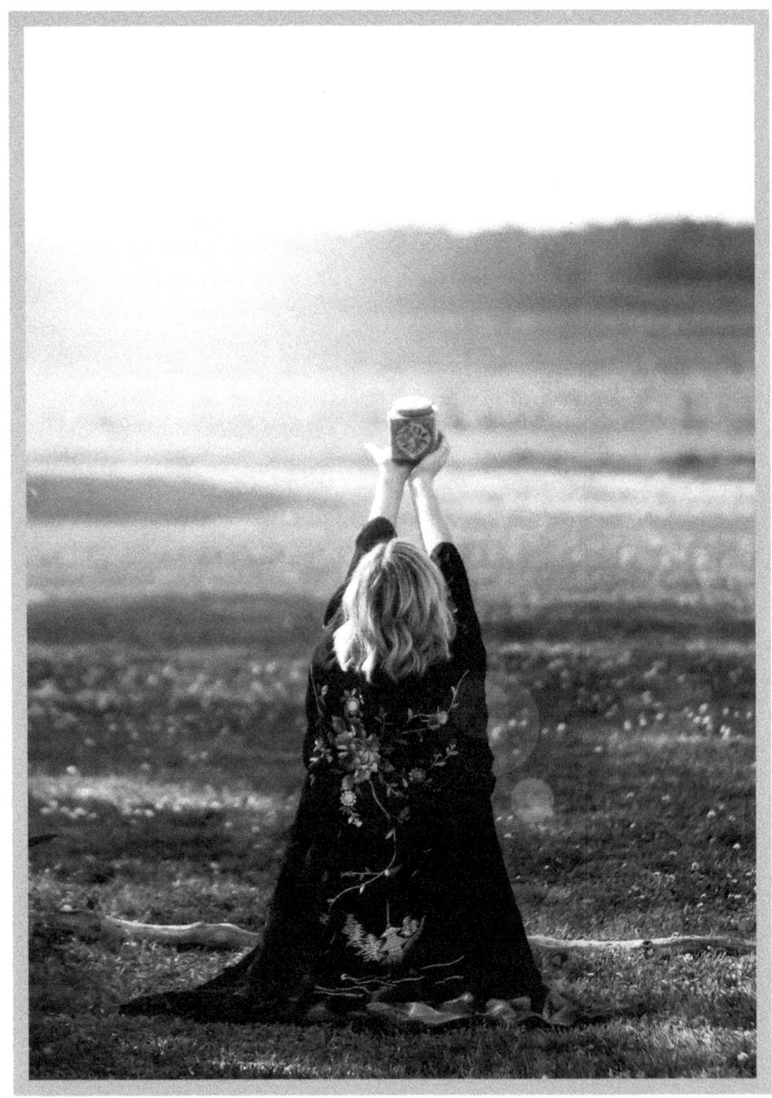

RESURRECTION

Bound by this
anxious wanting

I capture grief
in a jar-tight lid

watch it clamor
                                        gasp

the sound
that surrounds me

Today I open the lid
and watch it go

If I had a single flower for every time I think about you, I could walk forever in my garden.

—Alfred Lord Tennyson,
Garrett's Last Social Media Post

ACKNOWLEDGMENTS

Ekleksographia (ekleksographia.ahadadabooks.com), (2010): "Resurrection" (as "A Gathering of Bees")

The Louisiana Review: "Bon Rêves"

Snapdragon: A Journal of Art and Healing (Spring 2022): "Ode to the Backyard Dove."

The Southern Poetry Anthology, VIII, edited by William Wright, Texas Review Press (2018): "Metamorphosis" (as "Quilled in Blue")

Writing Texas, volume 4, edited by Lyman Grant, Lamar University Literary Press (2016-17): "A Mother's Grief"; "Choking Canary" (as "Avenue A"); "Learning How to Live Again" (as "Jackson Square")

Writing Texas, volume 9, edited by Lyman Grant, Lamar University Literary Press (2022-23): "The Sparrow."

DEDICATIONS

We would like to thank Christine Cote at Shanti Arts for her support of our manuscript. Our goal has always been to find a space that honors the intersection of art and healing, and we are grateful to be able to share our story.

Chantel would like to thank:

Emily Knobloch, for being our muse. Your image guided us through every step of the way;

My writing community, as well as those who create platforms that foster these communities that I am honored to have been a part of: Traci Brimhall, Mallory and Wiley Cash, Cindy Childress, Kai Coggin, Layne Craig, Megan Falley, Joan Kwon Glass, Charlotte Hogg, Ada Limón, Nathanael O'Reilly, Danielle Sellers, Cynthia Shearer, and Christie Tate;

My friends and family, for their unwavering support. From talks under carports over crawfish boils to walks under oak trees to laughter around the kitchen table, you kept me going during my own moments of grief in big and small ways. Kevin, thank you for going to all those poetry readings and celebrating the small accomplishments along the way;

To Karen, thank you for having the courage to share your story. This book would not have been possible without hours upon hours of late-night texts and phone calls talking about Garrett's life and sudden death, talking about your own grief and the will to live after his loss. Your story will undoubtedly provide hope and healing for those who know this indescribable pain.

Karen would like to thank:

Emily Knobloch, for your incredible collaboration and unwavering support. You have been an invaluable partner in bringing my vision to life, and your understanding, creativity, and dedication have been indispensable to me. I owe a debt of gratitude to you for being my muse, and for helping me achieve more than I ever thought possible;

Jim and Chris Knobloch, for graciously opening your home and sharing your family heirlooms that made all the difference in creating truly authentic and beautiful images. I am deeply grateful for your support and trust in me;

M Velasquez, for enduring the Louisiana swamp heat, insects, humidity, and even some acrobatics to capture that timeless image that we never imagined in a million years would end up in a place like this. I'm grateful to have you by my side on this journey;

Cooper Gros, for being my dedicated lighting assistant since the age of eight, skillfully capturing light and contributing to the realization of my creative vision. It has been a true honor to collaborate with you;

My friends and family, your steadfast support during my journey through grief has been my guiding light. Through every stumble, fall, and subsequent rise, you stood by me, offering unwavering encouragement. Thank you for championing me;

Chantel, my deepest gratitude for the incredible work you have done in helping to bring my images to life. Your ability to read beyond the surface and capture the unspoken words displayed in my photographs has been truly remarkable. You have a rare gift for seeing the subtle nuances that often go unnoticed and for writing those hidden stories with such eloquence and sensitivity. Your passion for and dedication to your craft has been an inspiration to me, and I feel truly fortunate to have had the opportunity to work with you.

And to all who have suffered the heart-wrenching and life-altering loss of a loved one and feel like their grief goes unnoticed and unacknowledged, we want you to know that you are not alone. We know that grief can be all-consuming, overwhelming, and life-changing, and we understand how it feels to be invisible and invalidated during your grief journey. Our deepest hope is that this book can be a source of comfort and solace and serve as a reminder that you are seen and heard, and that your grief is valid and deserving of acknowledgment. Through these pages, may you find healing and hope wherever you are on your grief journey.

ABOUT THE POET AND PHOTOGRAPHER

Chantel L. Carlson is an Instructor of English at Texas Christian University, where she teaches creative writing, drama and performance studies, poetry, and film/visual culture. She is a playwright, poet, and photographer. Her one-act plays, *Six Feet Apart* and *The Exhibit*, were published by Next Stage Press, and her dramatic scene "Distance" was published in *Writing Texas*. In addition, her poetry has appeared in *The Southern Poetry Anthology Volume VIII: Texas, Writing Texas, Unlocking the Word: An Anthology of Found Poetry, Anti-Heroin Chic, TEJASCOVIDO*, and *Snapdragon: A Journal of Art & Healing*. Her poetry chapbook, *Turning 25*, was published by Nouszot Press. She lives in Texas with her family.

Karen D. Gros has built successful businesses in both piano performance/pedagogy and portrait photography. Driven by a fervent dedication to creative expression and a desire to make a meaningful impact through visual narratives, she engages with audiences in a way that is both authentic and compelling.Blurring the lines between life and art, she reminds us that the world around us is a constantly evolving canvas waiting to be explored and transformed.Whether through photography or other forms of art, Karen believes that life imitates art and that our experiences are shaped by the stories we tell ourselves. Her photography has appeared in *Writing Texas*. In addition to her photography work, Karen is an Entrepreneur and Creative Director, with a talent for creating compelling images, messages, and campaigns. Karen is based in the vibrant city of New Orleans, where she draws inspiration from the city's rich culture and history.

Shanti Arts

Nature ▪ Art ▪ Spirit

Please visit us online
to browse our entire book catalog,
including poetry collections and fiction,
books on travel, nature, healing, art,
photography, and more.

Also take a look at our highly regarded art
and literary journal, *Still Point Arts Quarterly*,
which may be downloaded for free.

www.shantiarts.com

www.ingramcontent.com/pod-product-compliance
Lightning Source LLC
LaVergne TN
LVHW060628110826
845147LV00015B/959

9781962082198